The Young Scientist Investigates

Flowers

by
Terry Jennings

CHILDRENS PRESS®
CHICAGO

Illustrated by
Karen Daws
Peter Willmott

Library of Congress Cataloging-in-Publication Data

Jennings, Terry J.
    Flowers / by Terry Jennings.
        p.   cm. — (The Young scientist investigates)
    Includes index.
    Summary: An introduction to the basic characteristics of
plants and flowers. Includes instruction for a variety of simple
experiments.
    ISBN 0-516-08439-9
    1. Flowers—Juvenile literature. 2. Plants—Juvenile literature.
3. Flowers—Experiments—Juvenile literature. 4. Plants—
Experiments—Juvenile literature. [1. Flowers. 2. Plants.
3. Botany—Experiments. 4. Experiments.] I. Title. II. Series:
Jennings, Terry J. Young scientist investigates.
QK49.J38   1989
582.13—dc 19   89-37553
                                                   CIP
                                                    AC

North American edition published in 1989 by
Childrens Press®, Inc.

© Terry Jennings 1981
First published 1981 by Oxford University Press

Printed in the United States of America
1 2 3 4 5 6 7 8 9 10 R 98 97 96 95 94 93 92 91 90 89

The Young Scientist Investigates
Flowers

Contents

Plants and flowers

Plants with flowers can be found almost
everywhere. Many grow in gardens, in fields or
in parks. They can be found in vacant lots and in
woods. There are plants with flowers by rivers,
lakes, streams, ponds and ditches.

Weeds have flowers. Most trees have flowers.
Even vegetables like potatoes, carrots and
cabbages have flowers. If a plant makes seeds, it
also has flowers.

But not all plants have flowers. Some plants,
such as seaweeds, mushrooms, toadstools, ferns
and mosses never have flowers.

3

Parts of a plant

All plants with flowers have roots. Most roots grow straight down, but some grow along the ground, sending branches downward.

All flowering plants also have stems. The stems usually grow upward into the air and toward the light.

On the stems are the leaves and flowers. The leaves are almost always green. The leaves and flowers are formed inside buds.

Each part of the plant has a special job to do.

Primrose flowers

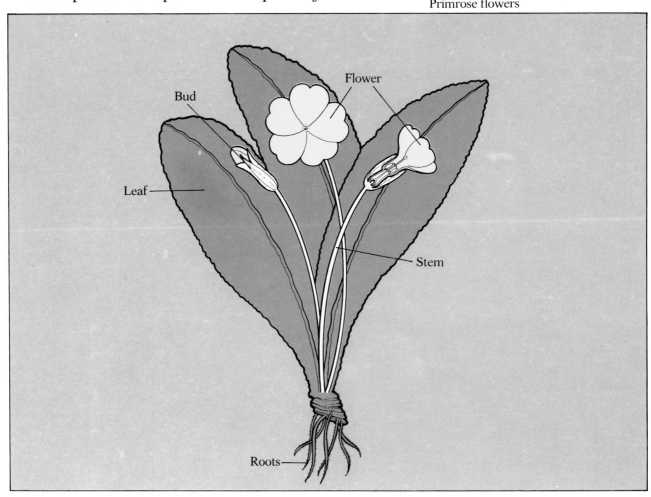

4

Roots

Duckweed — a floating water plant

All land plants with flowers have roots that grow into the soil. On many water plants the roots grow down into the mud at the bottom of the pond or river. On some floating water plants the roots hang down in the water.

Roots anchor the plant. They stop the wind from blowing it over. They stop animals from pulling the plant out of the ground.

Roots take in water from the soil. They also take in mineral salts with the water. The plant needs the water and mineral salts to help make its food and to help it grow.

Grasses

Dandelion

Iris

Stems

Climbing Bean

Bramble

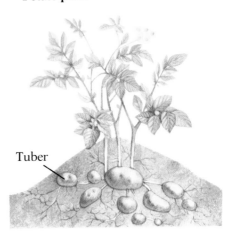

Plant bending toward the light from a window.

The stem of a plant carries water and food to all parts of the plant. The stem also holds up the flowers and leaves.

All plants need light. If a plant is growing in the shade, its stem will grow long so that the leaves and flowers can reach the light.

Stems may be long or short, smooth or rough, prickly or hairy, soft or hard. Some stems are straight, some twine round other plants for support. The trunk of a tree is a stem.

Inside the stem of a plant, there are tiny tubes. The tubes carry water and food to all parts of the plant.

Some kinds of stems stay underground. An underground stem is called a tuber. A potato is a tuber. It stores food for the potato plant.

Potato plant

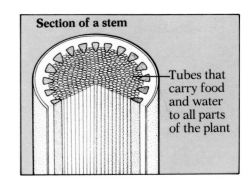

Tuber

Section of a stem

Tubes that carry food and water to all parts of the plant

Holly

Privet

Purple beech

Clover

Stinging nettle

Oak

Horse chestnut

Fern

Leaves

Leaves are almost always green. But sometimes the green is covered over with another color, such as red. The green substance in leaves is called chlorophyll.

Leaves make food for the plant. To make food they need the water and mineral salts they obtain from the soil. These are carried inside little tubes in the veins of the leaf.

Leaves also need sunshine and a gas from the air called carbon dioxide. The green chlorophyll in the leaves uses the sunshine to turn the water, mineral salts and carbon dioxide into food. Most plants do not grow well in shady places. There is not enough sunlight for the leaves to make their food.

Leaves have many different shapes. You can often tell a plant by the shape of its leaves.

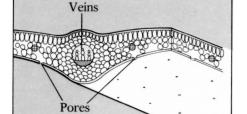

Section of a leaf

Veins

Pores

Flowers

Snowdrop

Dog rose

Wild orchid

Speedwell

Ground Ivy

Primrose

Foxglove

Flowers can be many colors and many different shapes. Many flowers are scented.

Some flowers are bright yellow like buttercups, dandelions and primroses. Some are white like the snowdrop and daisy. Bluebell, speedwell and ground ivy flowers are blue. The dog rose or wild rose has pink flowers. Foxglove flowers are reddish-purple and shaped like bells. Many large trees have small green flowers. The flowers of grasses are also green.

Flowers make seeds from which new plants grow. The seeds form inside a fruit.

Parts of a Flower

There are four parts to most flowers. These are the sepals, the petals, the stamens and the carpels. They are arranged in rings, one inside the other.

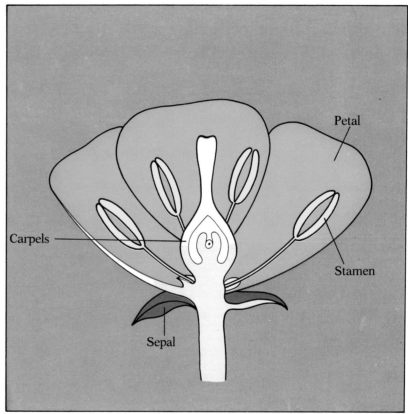

The parts of a flower

Quaking grass

Elm

Stamens with pollen

The sepals protected the flower while it was a young bud. Many petals are brightly colored to attract insects to the flower. Many flowers also have lovely scents so that bees and other insects will notice them and come to them.

The stamens make a yellow dust called pollen. If you shake a ripe flower, little clouds of pollen come off. The carpels are the parts of the flower that grow into a fruit. The seeds of the flower develop inside the fruit.

9

Pollination

If some pollen settles on the carpels of the same kind of flower, the carpels start to grow.

Sometimes the pollen is carried from one flower to another by insects. This usually happens when the flower is brightly colored and has nectar in it or a sweet scent. Insects do not mean to carry pollen to other flowers. They visit the brightly colored or scented flowers to feed on the nectar at the base of the petals or, if they are bees, to carry the pollen back to their hives.

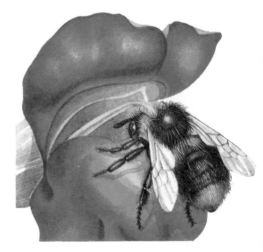

Some flowers such as the snapdragon are a special shape. As the insects reach into the flowers, the stamens bend over and shake pollen onto the insects' backs. When the insects fly to another flower, some of the pollen may brush against the carpels of the new flower. This is called pollination.

Apple blossom

Small green apples form

Ripe apples containing seeds

After pollen has been brushed against them, the carpels start to grow. Each carpel grows into a fruit, which contains the seeds.

Some flowers such as those of grasses and many large trees do not have brightly colored petals and nectar to attract insects. These flowers are pollinated by the wind. The pollen of wind pollinated flowers is very light and blows easily. Often wind pollinated flowers have no petals to get in the way of the pollen as it blows away.

If the pollen settles on a carpel of the same kind of flower as that from which it came, the carpel starts to grow into a fruit. The fruit has seeds in it.

Grass flowers blowing in the wind

11

Do you remember?

(Look for the answers in the part of the book you have just been reading if you do not know them.)

1   If a plant produces flowers, what else does it produce?

2   Name some kinds of plants that never have flowers.

3   What do roots do?

4   What does the stem of a plant carry inside the little tubes?

5   What things do leaves use to make food for the plant?

6   What are the flowers of grasses and many large trees like?

7   What are the four main parts of a flower?

8   Why are many petals brightly colored?

9   Where is pollen made and what does it look like?

10   What does the carpel grow into after the flower has been pollinated?

Things to do

1   **Make a flower collection for your nature table.** Collect garden flowers or the flowers of weeds you find in the garden. Place each flower between many sheets of newspaper. Put two heavy books on top of the flower "sandwich" and let it sit for at least two days. When the flower is dry, peel away the paper and glue the flower to poster board.

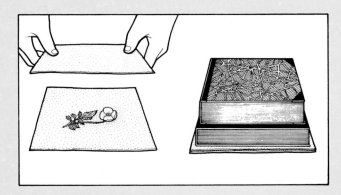

Label each flower. Use books to help you to find the names of any new ones.

2   **Make drawings of different flowers.** Do this whenever you can. Look at the flowers carefully as you draw. Try to color them to look like real flowers.

3   **Write lists of flowers that you have found.** Say where each one was growing and when it was flowering.

4   **Find out which flowers like different kinds of soil.** For example, some grow in sandy soil, some in clay soil, some in mud, and so on.

5   **Make a collection of leaf rubbings.** You will need some thin drawing paper and some crayons. Lay a leaf on the table so that the veins are uppermost. Place a sheet of paper over the leaf and hold it still.

Rub over the paper with a crayon. The pattern of the leaf will show on the paper.

Cut out the leaf rubbing and stick it in a book or on a sheet of poster board. Write about each of your leaf rubbings.

6   Make a graph to show how tall the flowers in your garden grow. The graph has been started for you. Copy it onto graph paper and finish it. Paste it into your book.

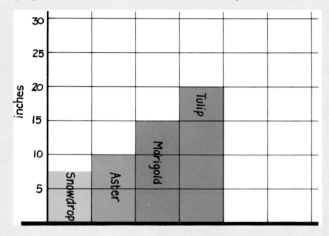

7   Pretend that you are standing in a forest in May. The leaf buds on the trees are just bursting. The ground is covered with a mass of bluebells. Think about what you can see.

Are the bluebell flowers moving? Is the sun shining through the trees? Can you hear the breeze rustling through the trees? What other sounds can you hear? Think about how you feel. Does the sight of the bluebells make you sad or happy?

Write a poem about the bluebells. Some these words might help you:

blue	delicate	rustling	cheerful
swaying	gentle	nodding	carpet
shining	restless	whispering	sorrow

8   Make a flower scrapbook. Obtain some old magazines and seed catalogs. Cut out any pictures of flowers you find to put in your scrapbook.

9   Write a story about how a flower got its name. Some flowers have unusual or funny names. Forget-me-not, foxglove, speedwell, thrift, Dutchman's breeches, black-eyed Susan, jack-in-the-pulpit, and Venus's-flytrap are just a few examples.

Choose a plant with a name you think is interesting and write a story about how it might have got its name. You might like to make up some music and movement to go with your story.

10   Study the stems of different plants. Find three or four large stems from different plants. Cut a piece from each stem about 2 inches long. Ask a grown-up to trim your stems so that the cut ends are flat.

Feel the cut ends of the stems. Are they wet or dry? Are they soft inside or are they hard? Is the stem solid or hollow? Look at the cut ends of the stems through a magnifying glass.

Press the cut ends of the stems into an inked pad or some fairly thick poster paint. Make a pattern with cut-stem prints on a sheet of clean paper.

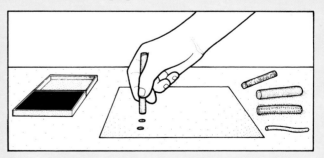

Garden flowers

On this page you can see pictures of some flowers that a gardener might grow.

Flowers grow in different ways. Some, such as peonies, iris, chrysanthemums, violets and primroses, grow on the same plant year after year. They are called perennials.

Other flowers, like petunias, marigolds, larkspur, candytuft and asters, usually die in the winter. New seeds must be sown next year. These plants that only flower once, the year the seeds are sown, are called annuals.

Pansies and sweet williams are sown one year, but the flowers come out the following year. These are called biennials.

Then, as we have already seen, some flowers grow on bushes and trees. They flower every year once the bush or tree has become big enough. Trees and bushes are perennials.

Michaelmas daisy

Larkspur

Poppy

Violet

French marigold

Sweet william

Wallflower

Candytuft

Chrysanthemum

Buttercups

The buttercup is a perennial. It flowers year after year from April to October. Buttercups are common plants in vacant lots, in meadows and by the roadside.

This is a buttercup flower. Some of the petals have been taken away to show the parts inside.

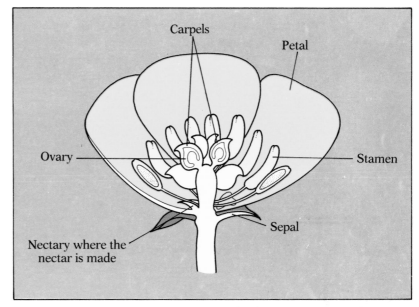

Carpels

Petal

Ovary

Stamen

Nectary where the nectar is made

Sepal

On the outside there are usually five green sepals. These protect the flower when it is a young bud. A buttercup has five yellow petals. At the bottom of each petal is a little cup that makes sweet nectar for the insects.

Inside the petals there are many stamens. Pollen is made in the little swelling at the top of each stamen.

In the middle of the flower are the carpels. At the bottom of each carpel there is an ovary. This is where the seeds develop.

Seeds and bulbs

Some plants, such as daffodils and tulips, have only one flower at the top of their stems. Other plants, including the buttercup, have more than one flower on each stem.

Tulip

Daffodil

Foxglove

16

Bluebell flowers

Bluebells in a forest

Bluebell bulbs

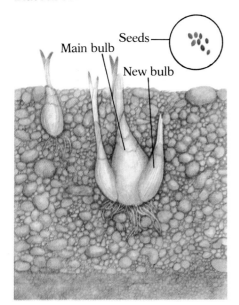

Seeds

Main bulb

New bulb

A bluebell has several bell-like flowers hanging from each stem. Bluebell flowers can be found in woods and parks from April to June. When the flowers have died away, small dry fruits are formed. Tiny black seeds are contained within the fruits. It takes about three years for a bluebell plant to grow from a seed.

But the bluebell also has another way of forming new plants. At the base of the bluebell stem is a bulb. Smaller bulbs grow from the main bulb. These tiny bulbs break away and grow to form new bluebell plants.

17

Bulbs and corms

Daffodils and hyacinths in a park

Hyacinths in a garden

Some of our most beautiful garden flowers grow from bulbs. They include daffodils, tulips, snowdrops and hyacinths. All of these plants flower in the spring. The bulbs are planted in the autumn. During the winter they grow very slowly. But when the weather becomes warmer, the bulbs grow quickly. The roots and leaves grow longer. And then flowers are formed.

Crocus

The food that makes the roots, leaves and flowers grow is inside the bulb. If you cut a bulb in half you can see the food. The food is stored in layers inside the bulb. A bulb is really a great big bud.

Did you know that an onion is also a bulb? It is made up of layers like a flower bulb. If an onion is left in the garden it will produce flowers.

Crocuses grow from things called corms. A corm looks like a bulb but it is not made up of layers inside. A corm is solid inside. A new corm grows on top of the old one.

Daffodil bulb cut in half

Crocus corm

New corm

Insects and flowers

Some flowers cannot be pollinated unless they are visited by certain kinds of insects with long tongues. Some of these insects with long tongues are bees, moths and butterflies.

In this picture a bumblebee has its long tongue down the tube of a white deadnettle flower. The bee is sipping nectar. As it does so, the stamens shed their yellow pollen on the bee's back. When the bee goes to another deadnettle flower to get more nectar, some of the pollen may stick on the carpels. Then the carpels start to grow.

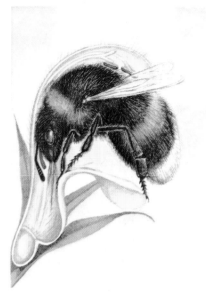

Bumblebee and white deadnettle

The long, trumpet-shaped flowers of honeysuckle have nectar deep inside the tube. The nectar can only be reached by some moths with very long tongues. When a moth goes after the nectar, some honeysuckle pollen may stick to its hairy body. If the moth then visits another honeysuckle flower, some of the pollen may brush against the carpels. Then the carpels can start to grow and make seeds.

Honeysuckle flower and moth

20

Daisies

Daisies are flowers with a round yellow center. Many petals grow around the center. Some daisies are annual and some are perennial.

The flower on a daisy plant is not really one flower. It is very many small flowers, called florets, joined together. In the middle of the daisy flower is a yellow part, like a small pincushion. Each of the little "pins" is a small flower called a tube floret.

On the outside of the daisy flower are small flowers, each with a white petal on it. These are called ray florets. There can be as many as 250 florets in one daisy flower.

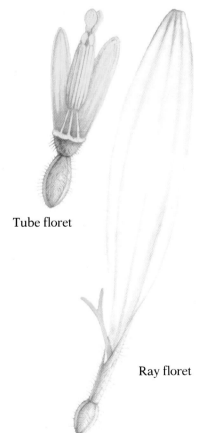

Tube floret

Ray floret

Dandelions

Dandelions grow almost everywhere in the town and in the country. They are in flower from April to October.

Like the daisy, the dandelion flower is not really one flower. It is hundreds of florets joined together. But, unlike the daisy flower, the dandelion has only ray florets, each with a yellow petal on it.

When the dandelion florets have died, white fluffy balls are left. People often call the white fluffy balls dandelion blowballs. These are really many tiny seeds, each with its own downy parachute.

Many other plants have their flowers made up of tiny florets. The thistle, coltsfoot, marigold and chrysanthemum are just a few. They, and many others whose flowers are made up of florets, are the biggest family of flowering plants in the world.

Ray floret

Dandelion blowball

Grasses

Grasses grow everywhere. They grow in large numbers in fields and on lawns. Grasses make the countryside green. Grasses flower in summertime.

There are pictures of some common grass flowers on this page. They look different from the other flowers we have seen so far in this book. They do not have brightly colored petals, but they do have stamens and carpels and can make little seeds.

Insects do not visit grass flowers. The wind blows yellow pollen onto the carpels of other grass flowers. Then the seeds start to form inside the carpels.

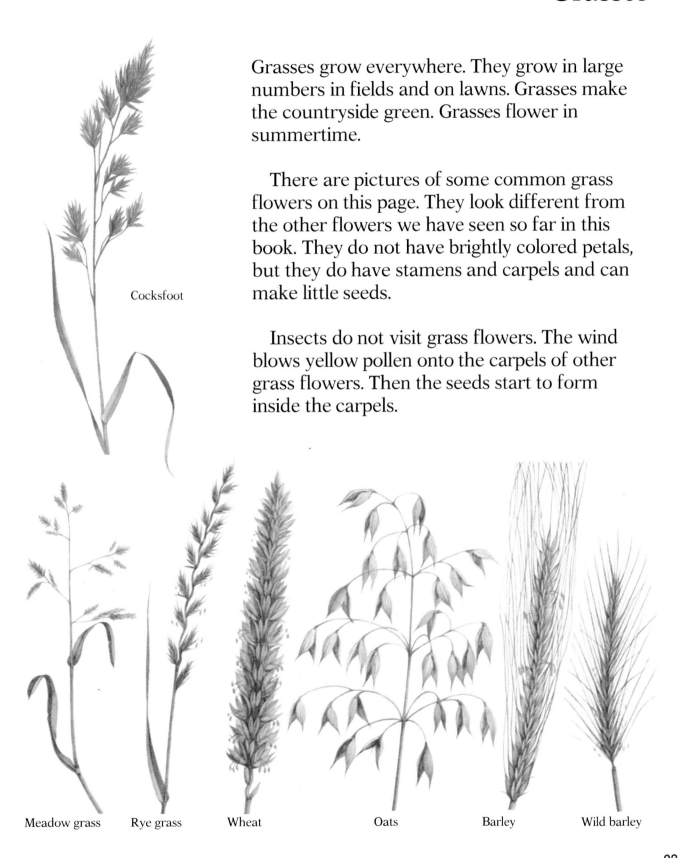

Cocksfoot

Meadow grass   Rye grass   Wheat   Oats   Barley   Wild barley

The hazel tree

The hazel tree carries its catkins early in the year. The catkins, which are the hazel flowers, are often to be found in January or February. They are there long before the tree has leaves.

The hazel tree has two kinds of flowers. The long, yellow catkins give off the pollen. The pollen is so light that it floats in the wind and may be carried far from the tree.

Female flower

Male flower (catkin)

Hazel pollen blows onto the red female flowers

If you look carefully among the hazel twigs, you will find the little red female flowers. When hazel pollen blows onto the red female flowers, they begin to grow into hazelnuts. Inside the nut is the seed from which a new hazel tree can grow.

Many other trees besides the hazel, including pussy willow, oak and ash, have catkins that are wind pollinated.

Small green hazelnuts are formed

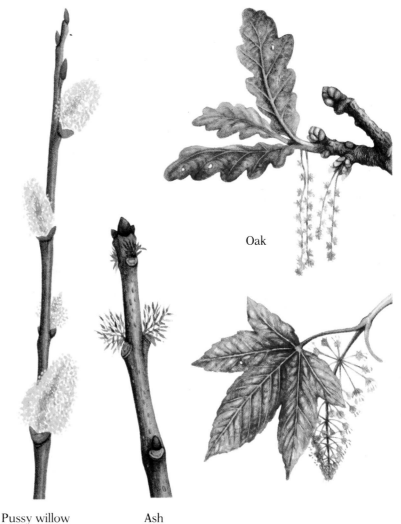

Oak

The nuts grow and ripen

Pussy willow   Ash

Do you remember?

1   How many times does an annual plant flower?

2   When does a perennial plant flower?

3   What is there at the bottom of the petal of a buttercup flower, and what does it do?

4   How long do the bluebell seeds take to produce a fully grown bluebell plant?

5   What other ways does a bluebell plant have of producing new plants?

6   What kinds of insects pollinate white deadnettle and honeysuckle flowers?

7   What are the tiny flowers that make up a daisy called?

8   How are grass flowers pollinated?

9   What are the two kinds of flowers on a hazel tree like?

10   What does the female hazel flower grow into after it has been pollinated?

11   Name four garden flowers that grow from bulbs.

12   When are bulbs planted?

13   Where is the food kept that makes the roots, leaves and flowers of the bulb grow?

14   What is a crocus corm like inside?

15   Where is a new crocus corm formed?

Things to do

1   **Make lists of the garden flowers that are annuals, perennials and biennials.** Look at a seed catalog to do this.

2   **Find out which plants have bulbs.** Collect pictures of them and put them in a scrapbook.

3   **Make a buttercup picture.** Cut out the shape of a buttercup flower in yellow felt or some other yellow cloth. Make sure that the flower has five petals. Cut out a leaf from a piece of green felt. Place the flower and leaf on a square of burlap or some other dark-colored material and sew them down with tiny stitches, or glue them down. Now embroider in the stems. Sew on, or glue, small pieces of green felt for the sepals. Put in the stamens of the flowers with yellow stitches, or sew on small yellow beads.

Mount your buttercup picture by sticking it down on thick cardboard or poster board.

4 Make a graph to show when wild flowers can be found. Obtain a large sheet of graph paper and draw in two thick lines. Write in the months of the year along the lower line.

As you see or read about a wild flower, fill in the square or squares when it can be seen flowering. The graph has been started for you.

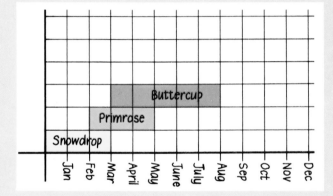

5 Make a collection of grass flowers. Press the flowers as described on page 12. Look for grass flowers in unmowed vacant lots or by roadsides. Mount the pressed grasses on cardboard or construction paper, using glue or clear tape. Use reference books to identify the grasses. Label each grass with its name and where and when you found it.

6 Write a story about a visit to a magic garden. Describe the flowers and wild animals you found there.

7 Make a book about plant leaves. Collect and press, draw or make leaf prints of as many different-shaped leaves as you can. Find the names of the plants from which the leaves came.

8 Start a collection of poems about wild flowers. Look for them in poetry books at school and at home. Copy the poems into a notebook and draw pictures to illustrate each of them.

9 Make sets to show where wild flowers grow. Draw a circle. Write down inside the circle names of all the flowers you know or can find out about that grow by the roadside. This has been started for you. Copy it and finish it. Now do the same for flowers that grow in the woods, in parks, on vacant lots, in fields, by streams, rivers and ponds, and by the sea. You will probably find that some of the flowers will be in several of the circles.

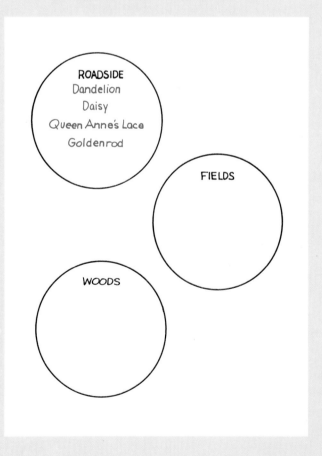

Experiments to try

Do your experiments carefully. Write or draw what you have done and what happens. Say what you have learned. Compare your findings with those of your friends.

1 How to grow new plants without planting seeds.

Sometimes it is possible to obtain new plants without planting seeds.

What you need: A carrot; a potato; some saucers.

What you do: Cut off the top of the carrot. Stand it in a saucer of water and leave it to grow on a windowsill in a warm room. Do the same with a piece of potato, making sure that there are one or two eyes in the piece you are growing. Measure the lengths of the shoots that grow out of your carrot top or piece of potato once a week. Make a graph to show how they have grown. Try to grow the tops of some other plants. Suitable plants to try include the tops of pineapples, turnips and artichokes.

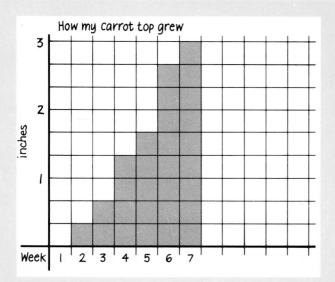

2 How to grow an onion in water

What you need: An onion; a narrow-necked glass jar.

What you do: Put an onion in the top of the jar. Keep the bottom part of the onion just covered with water. Keep the jar in a cool, dark place until the onion has grown shoots about 1 inch long. Then move it into the light.

Watch the onion grow. Measure the lengths of the leaves every week. Do the same thing with a hyacinth bulb in the autumn or winter. You can buy special glasses to grow hyacinth bulbs in.

If you plant bulbs indoors, keep them in a cool, dark place, such as a garage or basement, until they have grown shoots about 1 inch high. Then bring them into the light.

3 How easily do dandelion roots grow?

What you need: A dandelion plant dug up from the garden or from a vacant lot; three pots of moist potting soil.

What you do: Carefully cut three pieces off the root of the dandelion plant, each about 1 inch long. Notice which end of each piece of root was nearest the leaves.

Carefully plant each of your pieces of dandelion root, one in each pot. Plant the pieces just under the surface of the soil. Plant one piece the right way up (that is to say, the same way as it was growing on the original plant), another piece upside down, and the third piece on its side.

Keep the soil in the pots moist. Record carefully what happens to each of the three pieces of dandelion root. Do you know now why dandelions are such troublesome weeds in the garden?

Do the experiment again with pieces of dandelion root only 1/2 inch long. What is the smallest piece of dandelion root you can get to grow? How many new dandelion plants can you get to grow from the roots of one plant? Did you know that some people like to eat the leaves of fresh young dandelion plants, like those you have grown, in salads? They are very good for you!

4   What happens to drooping flowers in water?

What you need: Some drooping flowers; a jar of water.

What you do: Put the flowers in the jar of water and leave them for some time. What happens to the stems, the leaves and the flowers?

Draw the flowers when you first put them in the water. Draw them again each hour afterwards for three or four hours, to show what happens.

5   How much water does a plant use in a day?

Marigold is a good plant to use for this experiment.

What you need: A marigold plant dug up from the ground; a long-necked bottle; some plastic wrap; a plastic bag.

What you do: Carefully wash the marigold roots clean with cold water. Stand the plant in the bottle. Fill the bottle to the top with clean, cold water. Now seal the top of the bottle with plastic wrap.

Place the bottle and plant in a warm place and see how much water the plant uses up. Does the plant use up more or less water when it is placed in a cool place? Does the plant use up more water when it is in a light place or a dark place? Does it use more water in a drafty place or a place where the air is still? If you tie a plastic bag over the plant, you can easily see what happens to the water the plant takes in.

6   What happens to the water plants take in?

What you need: A white daisy flower with as long a stem as you can find (a common daisy, an ox-eye daisy or one of the garden daisies will do); a stick of celery; some red food coloring; a jar of water.

What you do: Add a few drops of red food coloring to a jar of water and stir the water until it is stained red. Put the stem of the daisy in the red water. What happens?

Try this experiment with a small stick of celery. After a few days, carefully cut across the stick of celery. Look at the cut end with a hand lens or magnifying glass. Can you see the small tubes up which water flows from the roots?

Try these experiments with blue, black or green inks and flowers of other colors.

7 Which flowers are most popular with insects?

What you do: Choose a common flower that is visited by insects. Record the kinds of insects, such as honeybees, bumblebees, flies, beetles, that go to the flower. Try and count how many insects of each kind visit the flower in an hour when the sun is shining and when the day is cloudy.

Now choose another kind of flower and compare the kinds of insects that come to this flower with those that visited the first one. Do some kinds of insects seem to prefer certain kinds of flowers? Make some flowers out of colored paper. Will insects visit these if you stand them out in the garden?

8 When do flowers open and close their petals?

If you study flowers carefully, you may be able to learn how to tell the time from them. Very few flowers stay open all day.

What you need: Some cardboard.

What you do: Keep watch on the flowers in your garden and take careful note of when they open and when they close their petals.

Some flowers you might pay particular attention to include morning glory, evening primrose, four-o'clock, moss rose, petunia, passionflower, moonflower and, if you have a garden pond, the white water lily. Make a cardboard clock and mark on it when the different flowers in your garden open and close.

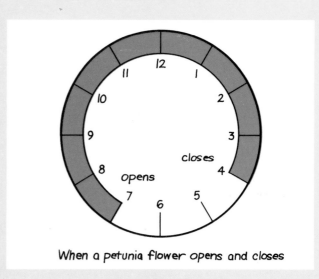

When a petunia flower opens and closes

9 Experiments with flower scents

Discover ways of making your bath water smell nice and refreshing by using the scent of flowers.

What you need: Petals from scented flowers, such as roses, dandelions, sweet peas, rosemary flowers or small sprigs of lavender; nettle or mint leaves; squares of muslin or cheesecloth; some string.

What you do: Put a good handful of chopped rose petals in a square of muslin or cheesecloth. Tie the material around the petals to form a bag. Hang the bag on the hot tap so that running water flows through it, or lower it on a string into the bath.

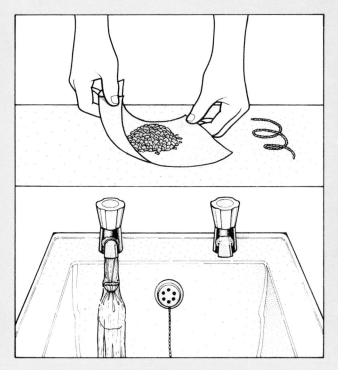

Do the same with other sweet-smelling flowers and leaves. Try these in different mixtures as well as on their own. Which give you the most refreshing bath?

Try to make perfume by crushing the petals of garden flowers with sweet smells in a little cold water. Ask your friends whether they can recognize which flowers the home-made perfumes came from. What happens when you mix two or three different perfumes together?

10   Study the life history of a garden plant from the seed to the flowering stage

Marigold is a good plant to choose; a dandelion will do, too.

What you need: A marigold fruiting head; some small pots containing moist soil (old disposable coffee cups, margarine tubs or yogurt cups will do).

What you do: Find a marigold fruiting head and carefully open it. How many seeds are there in each fruiting head? How do you think the seeds are normally scattered?

Plant some of the seeds in pots of moist soil. Keep the pots watered. Make notes and drawings of the growth of the seedlings. Carefully transplant your little marigold plants to other pots if they are overcrowded.

How long does it take for the marigold plants to form flowers from the time the seeds were planted? What do the marigold flowers look like? How many flowering heads does each plant have? Draw them.

Allow some of the marigold seedlings to remain overcrowded. Do they grow as well as those you thinned out? Does each plant produce more flowers or less than those that were thinned out?

Glossary

Here are the meanings of some words that you might have met for the first time in this book.

Annual plant: a plant that flowers from seeds sown the same year, and then dies.

Biennial plant: a plant whose seeds are sown one year but that flowers the next year, and then dies.

Bulb: a large bud that is planted and which grows to form roots, leaves and flowers. Daffodils, bluebells, hyacinths, snowdrops, tulips and onions grow from bulbs.

Carbon dioxide: a gas in the air that is used by green plants to make their food.

Carpel: the part of a flower that grows into a fruit and in which the seeds develop.

Chlorophyll: the green substance that gives plants their coloring, and with which they trap sunlight and use it to help to make their food.

Corm: a solid piece of plant stem that is planted and that grows to form roots, leaves and flowers. Crocuses and gladioli grow from corms.

Florets: the tiny flowers that make up the large flowers of daisies, thistles, marigolds, chrysanthemums and other flowers of the daisy family.

Fruit: the ripe carpel of a flower that contains the seeds.

Mineral salts: the chemical substances that plants obtain from the soil and use as food.

Nectar: the sweet substance made at the base of the petals of some flowers that helps to attract insects to the flower.

Perennial plant: a plant that goes on flowering year after year.

Petal: the part of a flower that is often brightly colored.

Pollination: the taking of pollen from the stamens of a flower and the placing of it on the carpels of that flower or another flower of the same kind. Sometimes insects take the pollen; sometimes the wind blows it; occasionally the pollen merely falls from the stamens onto the carpels.

Seed: the small object within a fruit that grows into a new plant.

Sepal: the small leaves on the outside of a flower that protect it while it is a young bud.

Stamen: the part of a flower that makes the yellow dustlike pollen.

Acknowledgments

The publishers would like to thank the following for permission to reproduce transparencies:

Heather Angel: p. 9, p. 22 and front cover; Ardea/London: p. 14: Bruce Coleman Ltd: Jane Burton p. 11, p. 21, back cover and p. 24, S Dalton p. 10; Terry Jennings: p. 4, p. 15, p. 17 and p. 18

Index